I0122722

At Word's Length...
The Creation and Manipulation of Conflict

By

W. Dale Stewart
Cover Art by: Sally Bomar & Tara Hull

The Brence Group
Maryville, Missouri

At Word's Length...
The Creation and Manipulation of Conflict

by: W. Dale Stewart

ISBN: 978-0692131459

Copyright 2018, W. Dale Stewart
All Rights Reserved

No portion of this work may be copied in any manner whatsoever without written permission from the author, except in the case of brief quotations embodied in articles or reviews.

*"Like apples of gold in a setting of silver,
is a word rightly spoken."
(Proverbs)*

Books By W. Dale Stewart

Where Life Meets Love

People of the Footprint

CONTENTS

Having Lunch With Cannibals

The calendar was the kind that had not only a little square of paper for each day of the year with the appropriate date, but a cartoon for the day as well. The date of the day is unremembered, but the cartoon sticks in my head.

The line drawing cartoon was of European explorers landing on a beach with their sailing ship anchored out to sea. The handful of explorers were met on the beach by a character apparently meant to represent a native of the newly discovered land. Dressed in a loin cloth and flowered head-dress, he welcomed the new arrivals with open arms and a big smile. His words of welcome were, "We're so glad you are here! We've been wanting to have you for dinner."

The cartoon picture showed a thick line of trees providing a background for the welcoming native. On the outer edge of the cartoon, was a clearing in the forest. In the forest clearing, out of the sight of the explorers, were several also smiling native dressed characters, standing around a large pot on a campfire. Floating and cooking in the pot were several human arms, hands and legs.

An invitation to "have lunch with cannibals" is not an invitation to accept without careful consideration. Getting "eaten alive" by others is not ever a pleasant prospect!

"Having Lunch With Cannibals" would have been a much more interest-grabbing title for this book. I have used that title over the years for many of the conflict resolution workshops that I've led. The title usually sparks a person's imagination and sometimes memory of personal experiences; however, it far too easily creates designated categories of "cannibal" and "victim." Often, when I'm honest, I have to admit that conflicts in which I have been personally involved, I have had a hand in continuing or even helping to create them. After several occasions leading my workshop on understanding conflict, I finally came to realize that the information I was sharing was not only to help the participants be aware of what was going on inside others. The lessons learned should also help them to be aware of what was going on within themselves.

In the late 1990's I was on an airline flight to Phoenix. I was traveling to attend a week-long workshop presented by the Alban Institute on understanding and leading a church congregation through conflict. As often happens, the passenger in the seat next to mine was quiet the entire flight until we began our descent into the airport. As we put away our reading material, she asked, "Do you have family in Phoenix or are you here on business?" I hesitantly replied, "I'm here for a seminar on conflict in the church." After a startled pause, she questioned,

"There's conflict in the church?" My best answer was simply, "Have you ever been a part of a church?"

Even as I asked her, I thought back. The home church of my childhood had several ministers during my years there. Several had left under unhappy circumstances. During those years, we were sometimes the largest church in town and sometimes one of the smallest. Since my father was a church officer and elder, I had overheard some of the conversations around our kitchen table when the minister or other leaders came to talk. The trip I was now taking was on the heels of my own leaving the pastoral ministry after many productive years in part because of conflict that I had helped to create. I wanted and needed to understand.

"Yes," was her answer, followed by, "I understand. Good luck."

In many corporations, the single greatest cause for the termination of an employee is not incompetence in doing the job but inability to work with other people. Schools continue to explore ways to address the rampant problem of "bullying" of and by students. Neighborhoods are gated, locked and patrolled to protect the residents from outsiders and often those within the walls do not get along with one another either. There are Domestic and Family Courts in the judicial system to handle families that cannot live in harmony.

In business, in school, in neighborhoods, in families, in organizations, in every human relationship . . . even in the church, there is the reality of some level of conflict. So, the question is, how do we understand and deal with this normal part of relationships?

Timing is an amazing thing! As I sit here writing, I just received an email message from a best friend. It was one of those multi-forwarded messages that the sender is sure will turn my life around because of the information it contains. This forwarded message was a long argument focusing on the practice of kneeling by some of the NFL players during the National Anthem as a protest. That act of protest has sparked political debate, Presidential profanity and Facebook tirades dividing families and the best of friends into wall-enclosed camps of absolute "rightness."

My friend and I disagree on the issue with no real hope of either one of us moving to wholeheartedly embrace the belief of the other. Yet, the friendship remains. My friend approaches the issue from one place and I from another. Yet, the relationship is not destroyed. It is my hope that he will eventually "see the light" and step to my side of the line drawn in the sand and I know that he has the same hope for me. Yet, even our opposite voting records does not diminish our common appreciation for one another.

The conflict element of our relationship does not

trounce on the absolute value of the other. Our disagreement does not lead to the name-calling which has become an acceptable part of discourse on social media. Our discussion and debate is not allowed to lead us into a disregard for the thoughts and beliefs of the other. In our arena of conflict, the momentum of emotion is recognized and not allowed to pull and shove us into a need for personal winning above everything else. These are choices we make and behaviors we control.

There is an old expression, commonly used to state the notion of protecting one's self by creating the boundaries and distances between people in any kind of relationship. The statement about "keeping someone at arm's length" implies actions or behavior that keeps a measured distance between individuals or groups. Most times, however, this distance is not created by our arms but by our words.

When I was involved in law enforcement, one technique that I utilized when interrogating someone, was controlling the distance between the other person and myself. Being within less than an arm's length of someone and "invading their space" most usually made them very nervous, agitated and defensive. That close physical proximity made them in less control of their emotions. And, to then move away into what felt like a safer distance changed their feeling into one of greater comfort. This was also true when I was working with individuals in mediation. There is an emotional safety afforded by an "arm's length." Words also help control distance and boundaries of relationships, determining emotional investment and safety. The words used can give a powerful clue to the intended boundaries being built around people with whom there is conflict.

At Word's Length is simply my sharing observations and a bit of learned understandings about the *momentum and manipulation* of conflict. By paying close attention to the language of conflict, the careful listener can begin to understand the meaning and purpose of the words used. Listening to my own words can also give insight and help me understand myself.

Some of the ideas and understandings shared here do not start at the same place as some other well accepted techniques for dealing with conflict. I appreciate and have used much of that understanding in training and mediation. However, my hope is that this effort will allow and even encourage a greater number of non-professionally trained persons to courageously soothe conflict with peace and brokenness with healing.

Noticing the Limp

May those who love us, love us;
and for those who don't,
may God turn their hearts,
and if not their hearts then their ankles...
so that we can know them
when they are coming.
(Irish Prayer)

How handy it would be if God would work the way the old Irish prayer asks. To see someone coming and know whether they were coming with something less than love and admiration in their heart would be a helpful ability to have. Sometimes a person's facial expression is an early warning alert signal. The tone of voice can give a hint of what is to come. But, what is often the case, a person is caught by surprise and what begins as a benign conversation changes without warning into anger or even accusation.

Sometimes relationship boundaries are in place for one person without an awareness on the part of others. On some occasions, everyone is caught off-guard by the movement and emotional change happening around them.

In the jungles and plains where untamed animals make their homes, the male of the species marks with its scent the boundaries of its territory. With the spray of body fluid, the lion leaves warnings to any other male that all that resides within these marks are off limits. As human males, it is not a general practice to leave our body scent on local trees and bushes to mark "our territory." Humans are a little more subtle when they do "verbal marking." What the male lion does with body scent, the human does with words. While the method is different, the intent is the same.

Several years ago, I was visiting a friend who lived on the West Coast. We had been friends since growing up together but that was the extent of our relationship. I was there to go whale-watching and enjoy warmer weather than was typical during a Midwestern February. During our outings to the beach, site-seeing and dinner we were sometimes joined by her male acquaintance. While my friend explained that their relationship was simply one of friendship, his comments to me with their implied meaning, led me to believe that his thinking was a bit more complex.

During my trip, when I was left alone to have conversation with her other acquaintance, I could hear and feel the boundaries being marked. Words were used to warn the potential intruder of boundaries not to be crossed. At the beach, comments were made about what "they enjoyed" when he took her to the beach. In deciding the place to have dinner, the discussion included the name of a favorite location when "they" went to dinner together.

Suggestions for sites to see were those that "they" had seen together. I wanted to tell him to just relax because I would be out of his "marked territory" in a couple of days.

Our human "verbal marking" can, in many instances, create definite relationship boundaries. Sometimes, our words are meant to create distances between other people. By our words, subtle and sometimes not so much, the length of the distance between other people can be marked. And, sometimes the distance may be between others and ourselves.

Manipulation...

Nobody likes conflict! Well, OK, almost nobody. Of course this concerns real conflict and not "entertainment conflict." Conflict for the entertainment of an audience is that contrived episode of yelling, name-calling and constant interrupting that can be seen and heard on programs of television and radio. Like a speedway car wreck or a professional wrestling match, some people are irresistibly drawn to verbal battles between people on topics from politics to sports to relationship fidelity. The primary problem with this entertainment conflict is that it may lead the listener to believe that what is broadcast is normal or expected behavior.

Surrounded by some of the brightest and most mature high school students, the question was one that almost made me laugh at first.

I was having an evening meal with students from around the state of Missouri who had been selected to attend a Youth Leadership Conference during their summer break. I was invited to talk about our professions and how what we did impacted our communities. I was involved, at the time, doing mediation for the District Courts and leading some workshops on conflict resolution. After explaining the basic education requirements for the profession and a little bit about what a mediation might look like, I opened our remaining time together for any questions.

Some had some personal experience with mediation as part of a peer mediation program in their school. A few were from homes of divorce and their parents had been ordered to mediation by the Domestic Court.

As our time together was coming to an end, the question came. The dark-haired young lady with a tone of sincere seriousness asked, "Is what you do fun?" Before answering, my memory glanced over a few scenes of recent encounters. I didn't want my reply to be harsh, but it did need to be honest. "Well, let me see. I'm spending a few hours in a room with two people who don't like each other, who don't want to be there and are there mainly because someone ordered them to and they have to pay money to me. Plus, I am trying to help them devise and agree to a solution about one of the most important things in their lives when if they were able to agree with one another, they might not be there in the first place. No, I don't think that would be at the top of my list of 'Fun Things to Do Today'," was my best answer to her question. I went on to explain that it was difficult, frustrating, emotional, exhausting and sometimes borderline threatening. However, that being said, it was also important and could be meaningful, life changing and make a difference in the lives of not only those in the room but other relationships as well.*

Dealing with conflict; fun, no... important, yes. It is not fun for almost anyone; however there a few for whom that even if conflict is not fun, it is useful and serves an end. There are some who seem to thrive on conflict. They have learned the ability to manipulate conflict to achieve their goals. Some have even become good at it.

A reasonable person might ask why anyone would thrive on conflict. What purpose could there be in keeping relationship waters crashing and unsettled instead of calm and flowing steadily? It is a common occurrence for there to be occasional conflict and relationship turmoil when people of deep conviction and differing ideas come into contact. When committed people disagree, discussion and debate can be filled with emotion and temper overwhelms judgment and civility. But in most situations, this is the exception rather than the norm; and the experience leaves those involved physically drained, emotionally shaky and thinking, "I don't want to do that again." In these cases, the conflict, kept in levels that allow an open-mindedness and at least in a small part a valuing of the worth of "disagreeing others," can result in a solution for a common good. This is not the purpose for the one who thrives on conflict.

For a few "conflict manipulators," they have learned that to incite and fuel conflict gives them a control that is like that of the third-grade playground bully. With taunts and name-calling, the bully can cause emotional and behavioral responses from other kids on the playground. The bully can feel the power of control as the victim of the taunts is "made" angry, frightened, defensive or powerless. With chosen words, the bully can isolate certain individuals or groups from the whole and establish categories into which others can be neatly placed. To create and control the conflict, the bully develops a sense of control over the other inhabitants of the playground.

The manipulator may also use conflict as a means of self-preservation. As often the playground bully lives in fear and self-doubt, the one who seems to consistently stir up the fire of conflict has learned how to shift and deflect potential attacks against self. Any attention that is given to anything negative about the bully or his behavior, is met immediately with a change of focus on the "badness" of another individual or group. The differences between those "others" is highlighted. In that way the bully changes the focus to the reason for necessary conflict with the "others." If the bully can fuel enough conflicts between different individuals and groups, there is not enough emotional energy and anger to go around. The bully is protected by the manipulation of deflection.

A secondary result of conflict manipulation is that it leaves some without a solid foundation from which to strike at the bully. Like trying to tiptoe on hot coals, if a person is having to "put out fires" from several points of conflict, there is no firm ground from which to focus on the bully. During football team practice, there is an activity that is sometimes called "bull in the ring." One player stands in the circle surrounded by other players and often with a coach also inside the ring. The player is directed to go after and tackle the coach in the circle, while the other players take their turns "blocking" the tackler and keeping him from the coach. Like in the football drill, the coach/issue/manipulator is untouchable because the player trying to do the tackling is occupied again and again with other "conflicts."

The one who manipulates conflict, even to the point of creating conflict, may do so for control or for self-preservation or often for an intended purpose. The manipulator may have a specific goal to accomplish which requires the division and separation of people or groups. Creating conflict can be a very powerful tool in social engineering, military campaigns, politics and even religion. The manipulation of conflict is ultimately about power and for the one who knows its language and use, a very powerful tool it can be.

The "Master Manipulator" has learned how to use the tools of the third-grade bully, but in adult form. The Manipulator will first discover a person or group's *fears*. These fears can be seen as the "loss of self." The loss may be physical, cultural, national, religious, financial or any other thing that gives identity to a person or group. A loss of culture or finances that identifies a person as "middle class" is equal to the loss of my "middle class self." When the religious group which identifies a person as associated with God comes into question by different beliefs, it can create a loss of my "righteous self." The Manipulator verbalizes support for these identifiers as the rightful possessions of the fearful person. In some cases, they can even be categorized as "God-given Rights."

However, rather than trying to dispel those fears, the Manipulator affirms them as real, powerful and to be expected. The *fear* then gives birth to *anger*. Like with the fear, anger is given verbal affirmation. It too is justified as expected, right and proper. To be angry is seen as the natural result of the loss of what is the person or group's right to possess.

The Manipulator will clearly identify and name those who are responsible for having "taken it away." Like the schoolyard bully, the naming quickly transitions into name-calling. In addition, the Manipulator will reflect the anger as their own anger. Whatever the individual or group is angry about, this *creator of conflict* will verbally be angry about as well. There is a difference though. The Manipulator is self-presented as not fearful for themselves, but for the others. *"I'm not afraid for me but for you and others who you hold dear"* is the image portrayed.

"Not only am I not afraid, I am the one who will do something about it" is the promise given.

"I'll stand with you, on your side, and we will make everything right... the way it's supposed to be!" And, there will be nothing to fear anymore.

The Manipulator has tapped into the other's fear, given it justification, and the fear has been encouraged into anger. The creator of conflict has personally identified with the anger, named those responsible for the rightful anger and presented themselves as the solution.

Yes, some people like, use and even thrive on conflict.

Language of Conflict

"The purpose of the meeting will be to discuss issues that are vital to the well-being of the organization."

It is a simple announcement and invitation that is guaranteed to not be so simple and may begin with "discussion" but most likely will not end there! What is advertised to be a time of sharing ideas back and forth may change into something altogether different, leaving participants wondering "what in the world happened?" Group conversation, that at the beginning seems to have a common focus and a respectful sharing of ideas, almost unnoticeably begins to take on a different life of its own. Conversation becomes laced with greater emotion. Personal positions are more firmly defended and statements of generalization and belief become like impenetrable brick walls. Sometimes, even the most passive participant can become caught-up in the conflict. And, the most disinterested listener can find almost as a surprise, a growing emotional investment in the final decisions made.

When the discussion scenario is taken out of the group setting and put within the relationship of two individuals, a very similar thing may happen. Friends or spouses can experience that same transformation when conversation moves beyond discussion into something else. That "something else" is what I choose to call "Stages of Conflict."

These **Stages of Conflict** are: ***Discussion, Debate, Disregard, Dismantle** and **Destroy***.

These five stages identify the movement of conflict from the benign to the destructive and from minimal emotional investment to overwhelming investment. By understanding these stages and their identifying characteristics, a person can track themselves and control their personal language and behavior. An awareness of the characteristics of each of these stages can give a careful listener some insight into the intent and behavior of those involved. A person can then choose to use words that can slow or end the growing intensity of the conflict. With careful listening to the words and language clues, the person responsible for directing the discussion can influence and change the temperament of the encounter.

(See illustration i)

Sometimes a person can find themselves unintentionally as a third-party in the middle of other individuals or groups that are in conflict. Even as an untrained non-professional, a person may be drawn into conflicts in a job setting, as part of a volunteer organization, in the middle of divorcing friends or arguing neighbors. On occasion, families have a member who is seen as the understood "peace-maker." Everyone goes to this person to help the family get along. They are expected to make family relationships all right again. Listening to the words is the key to knowing the intention.

Stage One: DISCUSSION

The first stage is what I choose to call **Discussion**. That's simple enough. People have a variety of discussions all the time as a normal part of human conversation. In a group setting, it may be a discussion about what color to paint the restroom in the building. While there may be differing opinions on the subject, the discussion focuses on an inanimate object – a thing. The decision made does not have a deep emotional impact on those in the conversation and the outcome is not long-lived. In this stage, the participants have a low level of emotional investment in the outcome. There may be differing opinions but basically the interaction between participants is about something that they can work out together. A consensus can be reached because it is not the type of disagreement that defines the worth of the group or individuals. An individual may not agree with the color chosen but the decision does not alter the person's relationship with others.

The language used in **Discussion** remains *"issue centered."* The words used speak primarily about things like paint and rooms. While decisions are being made, it does not matter so much who thinks one way or the other about the issue or basic idea.

The other noticeable characteristic about **Discussion** is that the language centers on "us" and "we." By this, the focus is on what would be the best decision for "all of us" which means the group as a whole or those who are even outside of the group. It is an all-inclusive "us." The kind of language being used focuses on the whole body or system including those people who perhaps are quite different from the discussing group or who may hold quite different opinions. This is language that can be understood as "All Us" in contrast to "Small Us" which is characteristic of a later stage of conflict.

Fortunately, much of our relationship differences involve just discussion and the issue is settled. But sometimes, our emotional investment grows greater, we move into the second stage of conflict and our words change.

Stage Two: DEBATE

In High School debate, the object is to make an argument that is more convincing than that of your opponent. The relationship is adversarial in nature and the goal is to win. In the stage of conflict which is identified as **Debate**, purpose begins to shift and there is a subtle change in the language used as well.

In helping couples learn to disagree in a way that

can be helpful to the relationship, each one is encouraged to use the personal "I" when speaking. The use of the singular-personal helps to state the wishes and feelings of the speaker more clearly. The use of "I" is an indication of the personal emotional investment of the speaker in what is being said.

In this second stage of conflict the use of "I" becomes more pronounced. It begins to be blended with "us." As statements are made, the language heard becomes "I think..." or ""What I believe is..." or "I want..." However, this subtle change from "us" to "I" is coupled with a continuing focus on the "Issue." The initial issue that was the original focus of the encounter remains at the center of the verbal exchange.

Back to the discussion about the color choice of paint for the bathroom, statements become:

"Well I think what we need to do is paint the room..."

The emotional need to have others support my idea has risen from a 1 to a 3 on a scale of 1-10. As I listen to the comments of others I begin to narrow my definition of "us" as those who do not openly disagree with me. It begins to be important for me to hold firm my position. Therefore when another differing option is offered, I am going to present my ideas in direct relationship or direct rebuttal to what else has been said.

"I think a much better choice is..."

In **Debate** the language still deals primarily with the issue, but now blended with a growing use of "I" and "me." It is starting to become important that people agree with me. The language is still centered on issue but I have more emotional investment in getting what I want.

As long the conflict conversation remains in the arenas of **Discussion** and **Debate**, the language and emotions are relatively passive and there are not too many long term difficulties. Language is primarily about "Us" and "Issue" with a little "I." However, sometimes a momentum begins to take over and propels the encounter into another stage identified as **Disregard.**

Stage Three: DISREGARD

The Regional Board of Directors of which I was a part often reflected very different viewpoints. But while differences were obvious and sometimes strongly shared, decisions were eventually made and we stayed around after adjournment for cookies and coffee. This evening's differences were obvious and expressed in a clearly noticeable way. As one point of information was shared by a board member, there was a change in language accompanied by firm nodding in agreement by a group sitting together. When a differing idea was offered, a firm negative shaking of heads was the response. In addition, the original speaker's body posture was toward the front of his chair, leaning into the group anxiously awaiting the moment's pause which allowed him to reassert himself into the disagreement.

As he spoke, his words focused much more on the speaker than the issue being spoken about. In introducing his comments, he began with a description of himself.

> *"I have been a part of this Region since its beginning and have served on this Board for over 10 years. I have led several committees and have owned a successful business here for years. My whole family has worked in this area... and what I think we need to do is..."*

It was enlightening to hear a differing speaker recognize the verbal ammunition being used. He responded by saying, "Well, I'm an attorney and have served on this Board for about 10 years; and I could go on about who I am, but I figure the truth is the truth no matter who says it, so I think..."

The stage of **Disregard** is identified by a very important shift in purpose and the language used. In this stage, the purpose of some or maybe even many of the participants is much more about being personally affirmed and "winning the day" than the specific issue. Statements of disagreement are centered almost completely on what "I think" and the evidence shared is a comparison of me to those who think differently. The language reflects a devaluing of not just the other person's beliefs but of the other person. The ideas of another person or group should be disregarded not on their merit alone but because of who holds the idea. The speaker gains affirmation of who they are by diminishing the value of anyone who disagrees.

Sometimes, the implication is that longevity or history gives a person and therefore their position more value.

"You know, I've been around for 47 years..."
" My father started this place..."
"I was here the last time we tried something like that, and..."
"I've learned over the years..."

Having a special knowledge or experience can be the difference between opposing views and people. The use of the simple phrase "I know..." can imply an indisputable knowledge that others do not have. Using language that says I have a special knowledge that another does not have, is to discount the value of anything or anyone that has no such knowledge.

Indications that the conflict has moved beyond **Discussion** and **Debate** can also be seen in interruption. Not allowing another person to complete their statement of belief or opinion is not just a simple act of poor manners but is disregarding the worth of the speaker. When compared to what the interrupter has to say, the conflicting statement has little value. It is what a verbal bully does to overpower someone else.

Another clear indication is the use of categorical name-calling. Any stroll through *TWITTER* or other social media sites reveals an increasing use of petty name-calling. From elected officials to the playground bully, assigning derogatory names to individuals or groups indicates disregard for the person and even for the issue. It has become completely personal. The use of name-calling moves the focus from what the individual or group thinks to what they are. Liar, Crooked, Sloppy, Cheeto-Head, Libtard, Snowflake, Loser, Dumb or any of the other names so commonly thrown around puts others in a common sack ready to be discarded as trash of no value.

In the language of **Disregard,** the speaker begins to center not on "us" but "I" and the "Issue" is overshadowed by the need to win.   With interruption, name-calling and statements such as, "I have been or are or am or I know..." the speaker gives evidence as someone who has an increasing emotional investment in the outcome of the argument. Personality has begun to take the leading role in the conflict. Who someone is, becomes the primary reason for whatever decision should be made. The language used is primarily to give credibility to the speaker more than a position on the issue. Credibility lies in who a person is, which makes what they say more important than any statement by someone of lesser status.

If a listener pays close attention, the "I" in the language becomes very noticeable. When the people involved in the conflict use this style of language, the conflict has moved past the first two stages of **_Discussion_** *and* **_Debate._** Groups, organizations and individuals in relationship need to understand that when the stage of **_Disregard_** is reached, a certain momentum takes over. This momentum of conflict moves those involved to the next two stages of conflict. This movement into a new stage of conflict can become very destructive very quickly.

One presumption that should not be made at this point is that the conflict will simply "go away" if it is ignored. Not dealing with the growing momentum of the conflict is the most common response to the discomfort that it creates. However, to do so simply clears the path into the next stage of **_Dismantle._**

Stage Four: DISMANTLE

Usually an election to the School Board of a suburban school district is not an act of conflict. It was different this time. One candidate's campaign had a simple and singular promise. "If elected, I will get rid of the Superintendent!" That was the total campaign. So, after being sworn in as a newly elected member of the Board, almost every meeting became an attempt to fulfill that election promise. Conducting the various pieces of school district business was secondary to arguing against whatever position was presented by the Superintendent. Every proposal was a launching pad for not only disagreement but personal attack. The proposal was not important because the language was all about the person.

> *"The Superintendent is only interested in a few families, does not understand the nature of the district, can not be trusted and does not tell the truth."*

Therefore, according to the newly elected board member, the ideas the Superintendent presents should be disregarded and he should not retain his position. Eventually the conflict became so personally focused that a physical altercation occurred following a School Board meeting. The member not only attempted to dismantle the Superintendent's reputation and relationship with the group, but his nose as well. The group had entered into the next stage of conflict that I call **Dismantle.**

Dismantle language can be characterized as moving from talking about issue and issue-person combined to focusing almost exclusively on person. What is commonly referred to as gossip is an often used tool to dismantle. Sometimes the person-focused language is a kind of "murmuring" on the fringe of the conflict.

During a quick break in the meeting to get coffee, the time may be used for a whisper campaign. The whispers seldom accuse someone of something directly but rely more on inference and innuendo.

In a conflict over the issue of money, there may be whispers about someone's personal financial status. The implication is their inability to make wise decisions about money. When dealing with a personnel issue, there may be whispers about someone's parenting of their children. The inference reflects a biblical mandate that aligns choosing leaders with their success as a parent. If the conflict is focused on long-range plans, there may be whispers about someone's tendency to change their mind often and quickly. The implication is the person who is so quick to change does not take into consideration all the important facts before deciding.

In these instances, the whisper left unspoken is that any person who agrees with "someone with those personal flaws" must have the same ones. The best solution then is to be disassociated from that person and that person from the group.

"I wonder if they would be happier just not being a part of this group?"
"I don't think they really fit in here."
"I think they have enough of their own problems to take care of."
"They create problems everywhere they go.

As the conflict becomes more emotionally invested, there may be an increased use of categorical name-calling. The negative names given not only says who "they are" but who "I am not."

"Outside troublemakers have no business here!"
"We have no use for ignorant rednecks!"
"You can't trust any of them; they're all liars!"
"If they can't go along with this, then to hell with them!"

In **Dismantle**, the language of conflict has a changed purpose. It is now about winning and even more important is the other person losing. The dynamic of win-lose becomes much more important than any particular issue. Before, the lack of "personal qualification" meant the *position* of the other person should not be considered and valued. Now, the lack of "personal quality" means the other *person* should not be considered and valued. The difference is subtle but extremely powerful. The conflict has become completely personal. The focus of the conflict has become the dismantling of the personality, reputation and relationships of anyone who disagrees or is different. My "rightness" may even come from a power or manifest destiny or even a wisdom bestowed by some all-knowing Godly Source.

Several years ago, I was asked to "sit in and listen" to the governing board of an organization that was dealing with conflict. The group of leaders began their discussion of a variety of issues with measured and focused attention.

However, when one previously discussed issue was presented, the language style quickly moved from Discussion to Debate and to Disregard. In the midst of several members trying to talk at the same time, there was a second's pause and one member spoke. "I know what God wants us to do..." followed by an unbending proclamation of the Divine's side of the disagreement. The speaker had a long history with the organization and was seen by many as the person who often spoke of God in the context of right and wrong behavior.

I have no way of knowing for sure the intent of the speaker. Was the position as "spokesperson for God" deeply believed by the speaker or was it a position used to manipulate the group into affirming the desire of one person? Whatever the intent, the result was clear. The statement was effective in drawing additional members to the one side. After all, who feels adequate to go against God's wishes? It also makes the argument absolute in such a way that the group gives itself permission to "go along" with that position even if contrary to that friend's or their own best judgment. The type of "preface statement" assumes power from history, hidden wisdom unknown to others or some manifest design. To begin with "Thus Sayeth the Lord" quiets the voices of most opposition. The careful listener will begin to hear the language of "us" once again. But now, the "us" is "us including this special power of which we are a part." The words are the same that were heard before, but the meaning could not be more different.

Moving from the early stages of conflict, **Discussion, Debate** and **Disregard** there is a language change. Beginning with statements that use "us and we" the language clues then change to an increasing use of "I." Statements of belief and desire are "I want, I believe, I think..." However, one important characteristic of **Dismantle** is the return to the use of the words "us and we."

"What is best for us is..."
"We think..."
"We want..."
"Everyone knows..."

Although the words are the same, the meaning of the "us" reference is different. In the beginning, "us" meant **All Us**. In this stage of conflict, "us" means **Small Us**. The words "us" and "we" now refer only to that group who agrees with me, are aligned in belief and support my position.

The transformed use of "us and we" can be an intentional and manipulative change. The intent is only to identify those who support a person with the original issue hardly secondary in importance. The manipulation of the "us language" also serves as a gravitational pull upon many into the center of the "small us." Being a part of the "us" is a comfortable feeling. It creates a more confident feeling as well. Most people are drawn to associate with groups of similarity. To put it simply, we like being a part of "us." And, the best way to know that we are an "us" is to have a clearly defined "not us." I know I am a part of "us" because I am different than "them."

In the 1970's, there was a marginally known and popular televangelist with a small following of viewers as he played his piano and sang with his "Holy Ghost" preaching. He was even selected by a writer in *Playboy Magazine* as the sexiest of all the televangelists. But, it was not his sex appeal that began to increase his popularity and income.

After coasting along with the growing number of preachers using television, his message began to undergo a subtle but powerful change. His sermons regularly included not only what "God told me" but also a consistent name-calling of anyone different or who might disagree. His favorite reference was about other ministers who had an academic degree from a mainline seminary, referring to them as "those cemetery trained preachers." His messages included the increasing use of statements as "believers like us," "only Holy Ghost filled people," and "the real people of God..." Message after message, the "us" became more narrowly defined and the "them" increasingly characterized with name-calling. As his language changed, his viewership and incoming donations grew. It feels good to be us!

Writing in 2017-2018, it is clearly evident that segments of the American population and electorate have been manipulated into narrow-vision pockets of "us" as opposed to "them" politically. With statements about a candidate's unique knowledge and ability and the blessings of some political-leaning religionists, a candidate may position himself as one who speaks and acts with an authority that supersedes all others. Mix in categorical name-calling of anyone who is different or disagrees, and a candidate can create an easily identified separation between "us" and "them." Verbalizing a personal anger about anything that makes someone else angry can then be added to the equation. And, through the intentional creation and manipulation of conflict, the votes and money just flow in. It feels good to be an us!

As already pointed out, one result of the process of dismantling is the categorizing of people into separate and defined groups. People can be "us or them," "for or against," "good or bad," "smart or dumb," "Christian or not," "patriotic or not" or any other groups that can be named and conveniently ostracized. But, there are other common results of this stage of conflict.

Another result of the **Dismantle Stage** is the leaving of the individual or group who are not part of the "small us." In many cases, the person leaving is the person in leadership whose reputation or relationships have been dismantled. With negative comments focused on the person, leaving is the political leader that loses the election, the minister who is quietly forced out, the coach who is asked to resign or the employee who is fired. The leaving parties are the ones who are made to feel they are no longer a part, those whose ideas are no longer heard and whose presence is no longer valued. While not always the leader, in this stage, someone leaving is virtually certain.

"But they will be more at home somewhere else."

The other result from the dismantling process affects the person who is seen as the "Trophy to be won." The person occupying the position of Trophy is often the person who historically holds power in the group. This person may have been selected to a recognized leadership position or simply understood by the group as someone whose opinion is respected. Many times, this person becomes seen as an ally of one side of the conflict. Any positive comment in response to any position is regarded as wholehearted support for the person championing that position. Therefore, the "Trophy", with or without trying, becomes a part of the conflict. From that position, they are then unable to affect a lessening of the conflict. The person is seen as either a supporter of one side or a trophy to be won by one side or the other.

"If we can just get them on our side..."

This person, as internal leader or outside helper such as a mediator, can be effective in dealing with the conflict in the early stages of **Discuss** and **Debate**. They can even have some success helping the group maneuver through the growing need to win of **Disregard.** But when the conflict is deeply entrenched in **Dismantle** most often there will be division and leaving.

Most friends of a married couple in the process of a divorce know how hard it is to maintain an equal relationship with both parties. One party will presume your support of the other with even the slightest positive statement made about that person. What typically happens is a loss of friendship with both sides. Trying to maintain a good relationship with both sides in the middle of dismantling is not only difficult but often unsuccessful.

In **Dismantle,** conflict can be used and manipulated by a choice of words to propel the group to an intended decision or even behavior. As individual members want to be associated with a clearly defined belief, they find themselves almost unknowingly drawn into the "small us." Identification with that "small us" gives a sense of knowing what is right and being right.

Unchecked, this momentum of conflict can carry individuals and groups into the dangerous final stage of **Destroy.**

Stage Five: DESTROY

In the previous stages of conflict, there has been a progression of language from "us to I" and back to "us" with a different meaning. The focus has moved from "issue" to "issue-person" and then to purely "person." The intent has changed from "reaching an agreed upon solution" to "winning." In each of the stages, the language used gives clues to the emotional investment that conflicting parties have in the outcome. The value of individuals that become categorized as "them" or "differing others" diminishes as the conflict progresses. In the final stage, the "small us" are not satisfied with dismantling the relationship of "us and them." The intent is to functionally eliminate the presence of "them."

Several years ago I had the privilege of having conversations that were eye-opening. David was not only a leading member of the Mayor's Commission on Human Rights, but also served as Executive Director of the Jewish Community Relations Bureau (You see how I give higher validity to what he said because of who he was). I asked him what I had thought was a somewhat complex question. His straight-forward answer took me by surprise. I asked, "What kind of hate could have been so great on the part of Nazi Germany to have created the Holocaust? How much hate does it take to purposefully slaughter six million people? How could this all be done by people who seemed to give the killing no second thought? What turned relatively common people into mass murderers?" David's answer was this, "It wasn't hate." He then continued in such a way as to say, "Hate involves an emotional connection to the act. That connection depends on at least a minimal value of the victim. The Jewish victims (and others) were seen as without value. The act of destroying them had no more emotional consequence than kicking a rock off the sidewalk." (This is a summation of our more detailed conversation)

While the events of the Holocaust are found within a larger historical context, there are language clues that reveal the creation and manipulation of conflict that played a part. A talented speaker, Adolf Hitler crafted his words to funnel a nation into a clearly defined "small us." His use of categorical name-calling and division subtly coerced even thoughtful people into "small us" belief and behavior. Some individuals, with political or racial intention and who understand how to use language, can be very effective in manipulating groups.

When Hitler's speeches of the 1930's and early 1940 are examined, some language clues can be found. He did not talk about what was good for him or what he wanted. His references were almost exclusively about the Volk (referring to the German people collectively), the people, the Reich and what was wanted and best for all. However, while the words were about "all us" the definition of the "us" grew more narrow. "Us" came to be defined as those of a certain Germanic heritage and Aryan blood. That group then became more defined as those who were a part of the political ideology that would bring about what was best for "us." As part of Hitler's rhetoric, what was best for all was presented within the context of a God created destiny for the "small us." And Hitler, with special knowledge and authority, was the one acting on behalf of this destiny. To disagree with this chosen one, is to oppose history and the divine.

As already discussed, an identified "them" is needed to clearly identify the "us." Because of historic undertones, the Jews became the focus. Other groups who did not fit into the characteristics of "small us" were deemed also "unfit." Much of this division of the populace was accomplished by the "murmuring." Accusation, stories and gossip were spread about what the Jews had done and were trying to do to economically overpower "us." In Hitler's 1939-1941 speeches, he called the Jews: infectious, racial tuberculosis, a criminal race, vermin and tapeworm parasites.

The crowds of followers heard the words, felt their own personal value and were drawn into the righteous destiny of the "small us." And, the words pointed to, dismantled and then devalued into nothing, six million "thems."

Now lest someone think that this momentum of

conflict forced perpetrators of the destruction to go against their will and responsibility, that is not the case. This is not an excuse for individual or group behavior. The behavior is not without personal choice, and with personal choice comes personal responsibility.

While the Holocaust is the momentum of conflict on a world scale, could this not also be the mindset of indiscriminate drive-by shootings, Las Vegas concert massacres and classmate killers?

During the past decade there has been much use of the designation of some acts as "Hate Crimes." I understand trying to identify the motivation of some destructive acts. Naming certain acts as a "Hate Crime" attempts to identify its cause as being the relationship of the perpetrator to the victim. This designation opens up additional legal liability in the prosecution of the crime. However, the "Hate Crime" label does not always correctly describe the motivation behind the act. More than just semantics, calling some acts a "Hate Crime" obscures the true nature of the belief system of the perpetrator that gives justification for the crime. It leaves out the total devaluing of another human being because of ethnicity, color, culture or nature of their sexuality. Sometimes this designation can hide the clues to recognizing stages of the development of a person's belief that results in their destructive behavior. To hear and understand the momentum may also open up possibilities for change.

Is there any way to begin to reverse this momentum of conflict and move it back to the less personal and more issue focused stages? Yes, I believe there is! In the same way that language gives us a method to understand what is happening, it also gives us the method to change what is happening.

In communication, we often get drawn into the language and behavior style of what we are hearing and seeing. It is similar to what groups experience in "mob mentality." Groups of people tend to mirror the behavior of what they see happening. The same is true of language.

Back on the school playground, one-by-one students begin to join in the verbal harassment and teasing of one of their own. Name-calling escalates in a "bullying one-upsmanship." That same game of "verbal follow the leader" also takes place in diffusing the harassment as well. One student says something consistently supportive of the victim and then another may mirror that verbal support. It takes only a few affirmations to change the nature of the encounter.

An individual may recognize the language clues that signal a movement of the conflict into **Disregard** or beyond. If that person intentionally begins to use only the language of Stage One or Two, others may be drawn into those stages as well. To focus on the use of the language of "Us" or "Us blended with I" may also draw others to do the same. A consistent focus on the "Issue" instead of the "Personal" may also help direct the conflict into less emotional investment. Simply engaging others in this "verbal follow the leader" by consistently using the language style of **Discussion** and **Debate** can draw others up to those levels.

"I think it's time to take a vote!"
    "I'm not sure the board (I – We) *has enough information yet. We* (All Us) *should give ourselves more time."*

"If you want to go along with his idea, I can't!"
    "We all (All Us) *appreciate all of your help and thoughts on the issue. Your involvement will be missed by everyone."*

In a group/organizational setting, the awareness of language is a vital tool for leadership. In a meeting, the leader can intentionally use language which keeps conflict focused on "Us" and "Issue." When "I" language is used predominantly, the response should be in mixed "I-We" or just "We." When the speaker is talking more about a person with an opposing position, the response should be focused on the issue. If a divisive action is subtly threatened by "Small Us", the response should be in the language of "All Us." An attempt to avoid conflict should not result in fearful surrender to the "Small Us."

The language of the recognized leader will be mirrored by the majority of the group. In meeting procedure, to recognize the stage of conflict can determine if and when to allow a vote by the group. In the two earliest stages, a decision may be made by vote with few lingering repercussions. However, a vote taken in **Disregard** or beyond, is a vote for or against persons more than the issue at hand. Those who feel they were "voted against" will carry with them a sense of negative emotional loss. To be a leader is often to "lead in language."

(Illustration i)   57

STAGES OF CONFLICT

Words	Stage	Focus
(All) Us/We	Discussion	Issue
We / I	Debate	Issue/ Person
I	Disregard	Person/ Issue
I / Us	Dismantle	Person
(Small) Us/We	Destroy	Person

Slicing Through the Golf-Ball...

I do not think there is anything more exciting or full of expectation than a wrapped Christmas present! Trying to discover what is hiding inside, we look and shake, feel its weight, listen for any sounds it makes and are finally left to make our "best guess" as to what is being shared. While that unknowing is fun leading up to Christmas, when the gift is a feeling or belief and the wrapping is language, the experience may not be one of joy and celebration.

What does someone do or say when they get a statement of belief dropped in their lap? What is a good response to a generalization? What about an absolute statement shared which reeks of prejudice and bigotry? Sometimes, when standing in the middle of opposing positions, the verbal gift feels more like a pissed off porcupine. So, without acquiring wounds, how can the quills be handled? Can someone say yes to the value of the person, and also navigate beneath the generalizations that create conflict? How can the issue be found that is hidden in the tangled mess of perception and power? Again, the key is our language!

For several years I had the opportunity to work with a variety of groups in understanding and productively moving through conflict. As the group found their places around the table, I asked them to do two things. First, I handed them a large, sealed plastic Easter egg which they examined, shook, weighed in their hands and a few even tried to smell. After examining the closed shell, they each made a guess of what was inside. During the years of using this exercise, no one guessed correctly.

Secondly, with a partner they were given a one sentence statement and were to decide what that statement meant. A few of the statements were:

> *"They don't want my husband."*
> *"All they do is spend money."*
> *"We can't get anything done."*
> *"No one respects women around here."*
> *"I'm the only person that does anything."*

As one would imagine, there was a wide variety of "meanings" applied to each statement. An incorrect meaning will most probably lead to an incorrect response.

In the beginning of my work with groups, before the use of the statements exercise, I was teaching a process of unpacking generalization with the use of story. Several weeks after a workshop, one of the participants shared with me a story. She worked with a group of teachers that also met together to share their religious faith. During a group conversation, one woman stated that she had stopped attending church because, "They don't want my husband!" The lady telling story could have dismissed the statement or defended the church or perhaps responded in a way that called her friend wrong. Instead she tried the story-telling process that she remembered and was able to uncover the meaning of the statement.

It was the practice of the minister of the church to send birthday cards to every member. The birthday of the friend's husband had come and gone with no card from the church. The progression of the couple's thinking was: No card received therefore no card was sent; cards are sent to everyone else therefore it was a decision not to send a card; the minister decided that the husband was not important enough to get a card therefore the minister didn't care if the husband was in the church; the leader of the church didn't want the husband to be a part of the church therefore "they don't want my husband there."

It is easy to examine the series of beliefs and presume they are wrong and even silly, but their power is able to determine behavior none-the-less. After understanding the "meaning" of the statement, the woman hearing the story told the story to the minister who discovered the oversight was the result of computer error. The minister then sent a card with an explanation and apology and saw the couple back in church the following Sunday. Unbending statements have powerful meanings but often the meaning is hidden beneath the words.

Those of us who play golf, but not very well, know what the inside of a golf ball looks like because our slice opens one up every once in a

while. Most golf balls have an inner core of hard rubber in the center. Wound around that inner core are yards of rubber string that cover all of the core's surface and enlarges its size. Covering the wrapped core is a tough and hard shell. The outer shell of the ball is all that a person sees.
(See illustration ii)

The same is true in the design of an individual's belief system. All belief is first born of *Event* which is then wrapped with bands of *Perception* and *Power.* That wrapped and hidden core is then encased in a hard shell *Generalization.* It is the generalization that is first presented. However, without unwrapping and revealing the core event, there is no way to halt the momentum of any created conflict.

An *event,* as used here, is a life occurrence which an individual perceives as having an effect on their life. That event is usually owned but it may be inherited. The owned event is an occurrence which happened to the individual "first hand." It is experienced personally and directly.

"A teenage boy pointed a gun at me and took my wallet."

An *inherited event* is not something experienced directly or first hand. The inherited experience creates an emotional response because of an a association with another person who has the first-hand experience.

"A teenage boy pointed a gun at my uncle and took his wallet."

With the ever-expanding news reporting and social media interaction, more and more individuals experience events of others and may develop a powerful emotional response and resulting generalization. A talented speaker/ storyteller can skillfully create an emotional response to an inherited event for the listener. With an understanding of the power of language, the speaker can intentionally create generalization and belief that results in conflict and divisive behavior. And, the same end result can come about even without intentional manipulation by speaker. Even an inherited event can be wrapped in perception and power and enclosed in a hard shell of generalization.

"Teenage boys in that part of town all carry guns that give them power to just steal anything they want from the hard-working, good people. You can't trust any of them. Whenever I'm down there, I'm going to carry my own 9 millimeter. Let some punk get close to me and they'll get what they deserve!"

All right, maybe that is a little too harsh of an example. How about something less violent?

"The last time a woman was elected as Chairperson of the Board, two of the men up for

promotion were passed over by a couple of women who got the jobs. I heard from the workers those women didn't know what they were doing. It's just the way women always try to take over everything when they get a little bit of power. I'm against having another one of them be in charge. It's just no good for us in the company."

All generalization and belief is first born of event. However, any event has meaning and thereby an emotional ingredient not simply because of what actually occurs, but because of the perception that defines it.

Most people are familiar with the "rope-snake trick." The idea is to use a small length of inanimate rope and place it on the ground in a coil, similar to a snake. An unsuspecting person walks towards the rope and upon seeing the coil, reacts as if the rope is a live snake. To get a more startled reaction, the piece of rope can be thrown or quickly handed to the person with the accompanying shout, "snake!"

The piece of rope is lifeless, has no ability to do harm and on a closer examination is recognized as not a snake. However, a person's perception of the rope causes the reaction. *Perception is greater than truth.* The person's response may partially be the result of a previous event that involved a snake. The reaction may also be influenced by culture. The saying "like a snake in the grass" reflects a negative experience with the characteristics of a snake. A belief about the snake may be formed by a religious view arising out of the biblical creation story in which the snake represents great evil. But the truth about the event is, there is a rope lying on the ground.

PERCEPTION is the internalized belief or evaluation of the facts and meaning of a specific event or thing.
An event may be what is done or what is left undone.
While it may in fact be truth, it is always more powerful than truth.
It is most often found in the answer to the question "What?"

What I believe you said or did is more important and more powerful than what you did say. My response will be shaped according to my perception of the event and not the event by itself. There are some people who with a simple greeting of "Hello, you look nice today," can leave a person feeling like they were just slapped in the face because of their tone of voice or body language. The hearer may be left wondering what was really meant by the statement or believe the statement was an attempt to manipulate and respond defensively.

Intertwined with perception, wrapping and covering the event is *power*. The meaning and emotional investment in an event is shaped by whether it gives or takes power away.

POWER is the exercise of influence (real or perceived) over a specific person or thing.
Power is always "fluid" and "unequal." It is most often found in the answer to the question "Who?"

The creation of my generalization and belief is often molded by decrease or increase of personal power. Most events that are experienced shape one's definition of self as having the greater power within a human relationship or having less. The "more or less" of power partially answers the questions, "Who am I?" and "Who are they?

My sophomore year in high school, I was on the basketball team. Now in saying I was on the team is to say that I sat, carried towels and helped the coach however he asked. The players on the team that year were good and led by a talented group of seniors. At the end of a game we lost to a rival team of a nearby town, the locker room was not a happy place. In all honesty, the referees were blatantly biased and our players were called for infractions ten times more than the other team. In an effort to sound understanding and supportive and to say that because of the referees we had no fair chance to win, I made one comment to a senior player. Looking back, I know my words came out poorly but the player and I knew each other, went to the same church and knew that I would never mean to offend him. I said, "There was no way we could win tonight. We lost just by you stepping out on the floor." I spent the next several minutes trying to recapture the breath that had been punched out of me. I had no breath as I tried to explain what I meant and said so badly.

Most people would use painful events as learning tools. Someone who is a "paid talker" would surely not repeat the mistake of choosing words carelessly. But, some of us continue to get our words ahead of our wisdom, so...

I had just returned from a vacation which included a Sunday morning visit to the church where I had been a member. At the weekly choir practice of the church I served as minister, I commented that I had sung with the other church choir on that previous Sunday. In answer to a question about what the other choir was like, I tried to say that it was similar to this choir. Like most, there are many more women in the choir and very few men. What I said was, " Their choir was a lot like ours... Light on men and heavy women." Once again I had to explain that what they believed I meant was not what I meant! Thankfully, the result of my words was not another punch in the gut. However there were some clearly written notes left on the pulpit for several following Sundays.

I am sure that my choir members must have

asked themselves the question, "What did he say?" What I said was not incorrect but the perception of what I said created the truth that was believed.

Events, owned or inherited, also have the ability to give or take away power. The event's ability is because power is always fluid. Power may seem to reside with a person in one setting, but not in another. In a business, the power to make and enforce policy may reside in a shift supervisor when on the production floor. That same supervisor may have little power when invited into the executive board room. The corporation president may have unquestioned power in the board room and virtually no power at home.

The husband and wife may sit at home trying to decide where to have dinner. Each one has a preference but neither wants to make the decision.

> *"Where do you want to go to dinner?"*
> *"I don't care, I'll go where you want to go."*
> *"No, I'll go wherever you choose."*
> *"I chose last time, your choice this time."*
> *"I don't care! You choose!"*

If the discussion with equal power continues, nobody is going to decide and they're going to sit home and be hungry all night! Eventually, someone will have to assume the power for that one decision.

> *"OK, we're going for pizza!"*

The power dynamics in the daily relationship of a couple or family are also played out in a much larger arena of behavior.

The selection of one individual over another to a position of authority gives power to that person. When they are perceived as representative of a group identified by ethnicity, age, gender or other category then the group is perceived as gaining power. Those who are not so identified may well perceive a loss of power. The power question of "Who?" may often be,

"Well who do they think they are?"

In our national political conflicts, the question of power is often a part of an inherited event. A dire future is promised because some group is identified as "wanting to take away our guns." The listener may or may not own a firearm, but feels power being taken away. When the event happens, power to protect myself, power to do what I want, my "God given, Constitutional right" will be taken from me. The event has never happened and most assuredly will not. However, the reality is not as controlling as the perception and change of power.

Young, professional athletes kneel while the National Anthem is played in silent protest against what they perceive as systemic racism. This occurs in a national telecast of an arena where the exercise of power is used to win and not lose. These wealthy young men, usually black, do not pay homage to the symbol of national power and personal identity. Without personally knowing a single one, the enraged voices of usually middle aged white men, answer the question of "Who do they think they are?"

"They're all a bunch of ungrateful, overpaid, punks that disrespect the flag and therefore the military. They should all be fired!"

A willingness to discuss the issue is replaced with categorical name-calling, a disregard for the person and grouping people as identified "thems" and "small us." The next stage is to dismantle their reputation and value, followed by dismantling their relationship to the group.

Going back to some of the original blanket statements given to the workshop participants, can an initiating event be identified?

"All they do is spend money." An individual volunteered to work with new employees as a mentor. Having been an employee for over 20 years, he felt that his shared experience could help increase production. Because production had plateaued, salaries had been stagnant for 3 years. His offer to volunteer was presented to the management team of persons with less than 5 years with the company. The team decided instead to hire a new 22 year old college graduate to develop a company "incentive program."

"We can't ever get anything done." The executive board of a community organization has had the same President for 5 years. By tradition, the President serves in the position for 2 years and then someone else takes over. The current President's father was a founding member of the organization. The current President volunteers to continue in office each year. Every idea for a new program or method is talked about and then the President never follows up or allows time to discuss the idea again.

"No one respects women around here." The 75 year old retired minister who attends church is always spoken of with fondness and appreciation for his caring. A middle-aged female member of the congregation says nothing in agreement or otherwise when his name is mentioned. On several occasions, when alone with her, the old minister has made what she heard as sexually demeaning statements. She also feels uncomfortable when he puts his hands around her waist in what others apparently see as just friendliness and support.

"I'm the only person who does anything." Two young women share an apartment while attending college. One of the women does all of the dish-washing. The other roommate is often gone in the evening and returns late at night after spending time with another person. One roommate is lesbian and the other is not.

Event, wrapped in perception and power, leads to a hardened covering of generalization. That generalization is usually verbalized in a belief statement that may do more to hide the event than to reveal it. In far too many cases, a person's view of life is reflected in the rounded surface of that golf-ball. Unfortunately, the reflection from a rounded surface gives a distorted view.

Many years ago I served as a police officer with a suburban police department. Both then and now, one real problem in police work is cynicism. Most cynicism is the result of negative generalization. During my years patrolling areas of the city, I was never dispatched to a home or business just because someone wanted to report that everything was going good for them. Virtually every encounter involved an event of hurt, crime or some type of difficulty. When an officer works in one specific geographical area and deals primarily with one specific ethnicity, gender, age or life style group, generalizations develop about that group. Since the events are negative, the group generalization is also negative.

"They were always arguing, fighting or complaining and getting arrested."

So what kind of perceptions are wrapped around the group when the sum total of the officer's experience is negative? Even if an officer has no event history with a person, if the person is defined as part of the group, the generalization applies.

This group generalization is especially true when officers do not have any other social involvement with members of the group. What generalization is created as the natural result of no experience to counterbalance the negative?

There is a common mindset within the law enforcement community that can be called "the thin blue line." It is the portrayed image of police officers standing shoulder-to-shoulder as that thin but powerful line separating good from bad, victim from crook, civilization from anarchy and right from wrong. The image is coupled with the idea that is heard in the ranks, "no one can understand an officer except another officer nor an officer's family than another family." While somewhat true, the image creates a "small us" identity and a powerful "us against them" generalization shell. It defines how one group tends to see and behave toward people and ideas outside of the group.

Equally troublesome is the exact same scenario that takes place within some groups looking at law enforcement from the outside.

"Did you see on television how those cops beat up that man just because of his color?"
"My cousin almost got shot and he didn't do anything."
"I have to carry just to protect myself."
"I got pulled over last night. They said it was my busted headlight, but I know it was race."

Any owned or inherited event can be wrapped in

perception of unfairness and power lost. The wrapped event then creates the hardened generalization about an identified "them." The group of "them" are all alike because they all look alike and all should be treated the same. The "thin blue line" perceived by some as all good becomes seen by others as all bad. This "thin blue line mentality" hides the common humanity of both and widens the gulf that separates them. While sounding to some as simplistic or naive, creating ways for officers to be seen as a part of the community they police, is vital.

Since this book is about conflict, all the illustrations up to this point have been about creating negative generalization. However generalization and belief and the responses they generate may also be positive.

Why is it that certain things are important to people in a particular religious experience? It is a belief system that encases our perceptions and issues of power wound around a particular event known personally or historically. We then develop symbols that remind us of the event and proclaims its current importance. The symbol then reinforces our belief.

So much of the structure of human relationships are these golf-ball events that reflect how people and groups are seen. These events, wrapped in perception and power and encased in generalization create belief and give permission to behavior.

Illustration ii   77

SLICING THROUGH THE GOLF-BALL

EVENT
(Owned or Inherited)

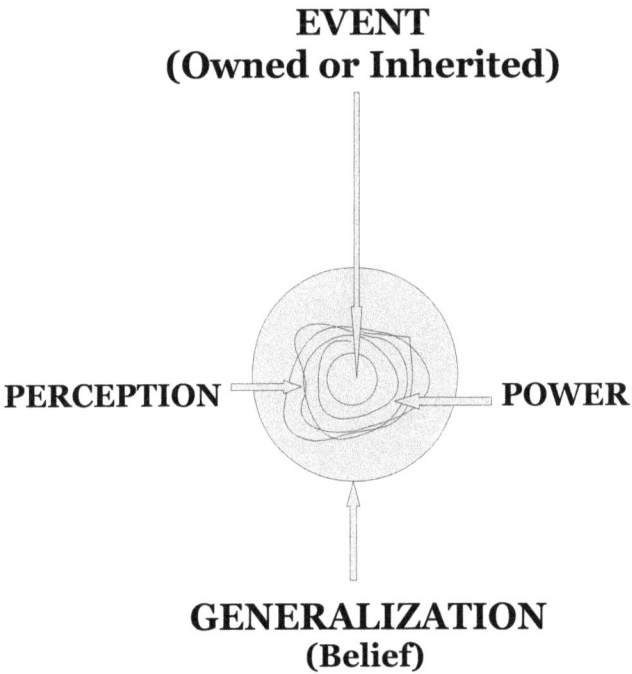

PERCEPTION   **POWER**

GENERALIZATION
(Belief)

Momentum of Conflict

Imagine a small tree in the yard that is just beginning its growth. The limbs begin to form and extend from the trunk. Two of these pliable stems grow almost parallel to one another. Sometimes a young boy would take small pebbles and place them between the limbs. The pebbles were just large enough to fit in the space between the limbs. One day, the young boy took a golf-ball he found in the yard and wedged it between the two growing limbs. The inside of the ball was the same size as the pebble, but the inside had been wrapped in hundreds of feet of rubber bands. The outside cover of the ball is hard and unyielding to the pressure of the limbs. The ball, now separating the limbs just slightly, altered the course of their growth. The limbs that once grew side-by-side, almost close enough to touch now began a path of growth away from one another. The further they grow, the greater the distance that separates them. As the years pass, the limbs that once grew along an almost identical path, now have grown in opposite directions. There is no place along their life route that they could ever touch.

The image of the limbs gives a picture of individuals and groups who begin together but whose life paths become altered into widely separated directions. This is the "momentum of conflict." Two sides are in relationship simply because of the common humanity into which they are born. No two people or groups are ever without some separation. They are both separated and joined by small "pebble events" of life. However when the small event is wrapped with perception and power that gives it meaning and creates generalization, the relationship begins to be forced apart. The growth apart will continue unless an act of intervention pulls out the golf-ball and helps the separated individuals to realign their movement and relationship to one another.

Without intervention and change, the conflict that results from the separation becomes evident. One person's vision of the other becomes more and more narrow. In time, there is nothing the other does that is interpreted in a positive way. There is nothing the other says that has any importance. Any attempt at reconciliation is seen with suspicion. As vision narrows and generalization hardens, there is "communication loss." The relationship then experiences "contact loss."

"I'm through trying to talk to them."
"I hope I never have to see them again."

Finally a point is reached where the other person ceases to exist in value except as an object that takes up space and time. Instead of being seen as a part of "manhood, womanhood, personhood" the other has become what I call "Non-hood." With a powerful momentum, the relationship moves steadily through the later conflict stages of Disregard, Dismantle and possibly even Destroy. (See illustration iii)

In churches and other volunteer organizations, there is a pattern to a member's gradual disassociation. Even in the midst of conflict and perhaps as a result of it, individuals will continue to verbalize their thoughts. They will continue to share ideas and options. Meeting no response that gives an indication of valuing what is offered or the person doing the offering, input will diminish and finally stop. The individual's presence remains but their efforts to openly communicate does not. Sometimes the attempt to communicate will change settings. The "parking lot board meeting" is called to order after the official body has adjourned. This smaller and unofficial gathering is believed to be "the only place I will be listened to." However, in most cases, this gathering accomplishes little except to harden the generalizations already held. It also further separates groups into "small us" and "them."

With the belief that the "idea and idea giver" are not valued in the whole organization, contact becomes unnecessary and unwanted. Some association may continue with the "parking lot board" but that just serves to reinforce a negative feeling about the whole. Hardened generalizations are held as absolute truth and there is no questioning their validity. Generalizations are no longer just about the organization's beliefs but the nature of the organization itself. If the organization has no value, then members of it have diminished value as well. Separation from the group becomes essential in order to maintain personal value.

MOMENTUM OF CONFLICT

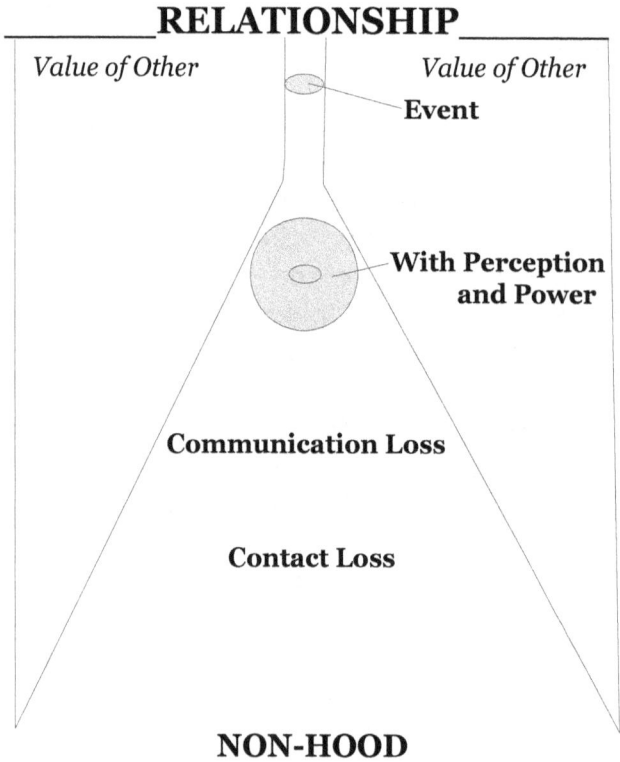

RELATIONSHIP

Value of Other   *Value of Other*

Event

With Perception
and Power

Communication Loss

Contact Loss

NON-HOOD

Perception To Prejudice

It would be wonderful if a widely held perception that devaluing another human being because of color, race, ethnicity, gender or sexuality ended with a corrective re-writing of the Constitution. Perhaps with the Emancipation Proclamation, the end of the American Civil War, the Voting Rights Act or simply a maturing of the human thought process also would come the demise of racism. However, it is a dream that is yet to be reached.

I am not acquainted with every person who currently exists. But of those whose paths I have crossed in a variety of locations, it seems all have a struggle with prejudice. In my experience, the greatest of prejudice centers on race, color and gender. Maybe that's because differences are so visually apparent and therefore hard to ignore. Perhaps because the culture in which we were shaped and molded has an undeniable history that virtually deifies western European accomplishment. That same history denies comparable value to any different cultures. It is said that "history is written by the winners" and therefore the "better than." It is not hard to understand that many of our perceptions and give/take of power are the products of that same history. Those "inherited events" of history are easily encased in a hardened shell of generalization and belief which gives cultural identity to certain groups. Our "owned events" with members of these "less than" groups are then reflected on and interpreted by the negative generalization.

Prejudice, against any group, will continue to mold thought and behavior within culture as long as those in power do not act unambiguously against it. In publicly portrayed and privately held generalizations, some groups continue in their "less than" and devalued status. Although the most obvious grouping is identified by race and color, prejudice also diminishes those grouped by gender, age, sexual orientation and ethnicity. Common language is filled with "all blacks on government handouts," "Feminazis," "senile old and the rebellious selfish young," "lazy Mexican rapists," "homo perverts," "white trash" and "drunk savage Indians." And, the persons in power have nothing to personally gain by working to change the perceptions and generalizations. To lessen the prejudice would result in a re-balancing of the fluid and unequal possession of power.

Just as everyone has their own prejudices, there are a variety of ways to deal with them. Some recognize the prejudice and allow it to be truth. It is seen as normal and promoted as a truth to be affirmed by all. Behavior is shaped and given permission by the prejudice. This group-held truth forms the core of "small us."

"I don't care what anybody else says, they ruin every place they move to. I won't let them move into our neighborhood!"

There are some persons who recognize and even acknowledge their prejudice to themselves. The prejudice may not be seen as absolute truth about people in every case. However, it is understood as usually true and guides behavior selectively. The prejudice becomes the guide for behavior, when it personally affects me.

"It's a free country and you can believe and do what you want, but I'll never live next to one of them!"

Thankfully, there are many individuals who recognize their own prejudice and consciously decide to not let it determine their behavior. Many of these prejudices are remnants of a past culture or history. I have a friend who was raised in the deep south and was engulfed in the racism of that time and place. When he served in the military, like often happens, his racial prejudices were challenged. That challenge created new perceptions for him and altered his generalization. However, even decades later, he knowingly refers to himself as a "recovering racist." He is honest enough with himself to know that often his first thoughts are born of deeply ingrained prejudice which he intentionally has to confront. His efforts within himself, coupled with his words have helped create different perceptions and generalizations for his children.

"That doesn't bother me like it once did. It's only right for them to have a chance to be good neighbors too."

For some, perhaps most, their prejudice is subtly hidden away. They have convinced themselves that they are not prejudiced. They have a handy defense against any accusation that is levied against them. It is a simple statement with which they can convince even themselves that they are never motivated by prejudice.

"I have a long time friend of the family who has worked for us for years. We treat him just like family. He even came to my daughter's wedding."

If I can point to one observable exception to the prejudice in my behavior, then I must not be prejudice.

The first real conflict I ever had as the minister of a church was about race. I had been serving the small congregation on a part-time basis for six months. The church decided I should be full time and live in the community so I had just moved to the city. Located in traditional cotton country, the city had a long history of tension between races. Most of the families of the church had lived in the area for generations. Like most small churches, the church had minimal resources of money or people. The one thing it did have was much more land than it could use, in a prime location. A decision had been made to sell a portion of the land in order to build a much needed additional facility.

At my first meeting of the Official Board, I was welcomed as the now resident minister and a motion was passed unanimously to disband the Search Committee which had hired me. As the meeting was about to adjourn, one member had one more issue to discuss. He stated that he "had heard" that a local real estate company was talking to a local funeral home that was interested in relocating to the property the church had advertised for sale. I thought it sounded like great news.

Almost in unison, board members shook their heads at the unacceptable nature of the sale. The mentioned potential purchaser was the funeral home that served the African American community (my term) exclusively. Members offered that "those people" would be sitting around the property all times and after dark. The church wouldn't be able to have night meetings or youth activities because no one would come. If the property was sold to "that funeral home" some of those Board members would stop coming. I just sat and listened, surprised by what I heard and from whom I heard it.

After a while, the man who brought up the rumored possibility noted that I had said nothing. The members looked at me and awaited a comment. I was younger and perhaps more *courageous than wise. What I said was, "If the Board decides to make a decision that stops the future and ministry of this church because of racial prejudice, then you probably need to put the Search Committee back together again."*

The Chairman asked if I would resign if they weren't willing to sell the property to that funeral home? I replied, "No, I don't believe in quitting; but I would probably say some things that would get me fired."

It all turned out to be nothing more than a rumor and the property was later sold to Taco Bell. But, it was an early glimpse at the prejudice found in a group of very caring, loving and growing group of people. The real beauty of remembering that story is that now, decades later, the church's minister is African American!

Through the years, good, highly educated and faithful people have also told me, "If an Asian person walks in the door, I'm walking out." An older black man with a PhD. joined church and a woman said to her friends, "He lives down the hallway from my apartment. I hope I never run into him after dark." Time after time, the prejudice hibernates until a present event awakens it again. And, in almost every instance, it is denied by pointing out, "Well, I have a friend who is Black/Hispanic/Asian/Gay..." or "Look, there's my African American" while pointing into the crowd.

In my continuation with that first church, I had additional conversations about the place of prejudice in our lives. It was finally, with a friend over coffee, that a simple new awareness came. The friend was again reminding me of an old black man that had worked for my friend's father for many years. He commented that the family considered the man as part of their family and trusted him to run the business during vacation times. My friend knew that he held no biased feelings toward the employee. I was sure of my friend's sincerity. But here's the key – the old employee had proved his value which set him apart from others of his race.

The difference is simple but powerful in its subtlety. Prejudice defines how a person or group is seen at the first contact. What perception shapes the relationship with a person when there is no personal experience with that individual or group? With no evidence arising from an "owned event," what belief guides behavior toward the other person? Perhaps it is best summed up this way:

Whites (people like me) are good and valued,
but some can prove themselves to be bad.
Blacks (people not like me) are bad,
but some can prove themselves to be good and
valued.

Prejudice, issues of perception and power wrapped in generalization, is found at the starting point of how I see and react to individuals and groups.

Telling a New Story

I know that up to this point any reader's experience with this book has felt like only one side of a "bad news – good news" story. The momentum of conflict seems almost unstoppable. Perception and generalizations hide truth. Even good people can be convinced to do horrible things if someone just uses the right words. Is the only option to run away in order to not be swept away in a torrent of conflict? Is the only good relationship one which remains so shallow that there is no place for honest disagreement?

This sharing of observation and experience is actually about hope. It is born of the firm belief that virtually anyone can have the ability to create a different outcome to conflict. Even if some conflict is inevitable in any relationship, the result is not.

Within family, work, church, volunteer organizations and even politics the average person can make a difference. It does not take a graduate degree or a magic wand. Making a difference does involve a careful listening to language. Listening can lead to discovering what is really being said. Making a difference means observing the behavior that is the result of what is perceived and believed. Finally, making a difference is pausing to consider what it all means for the people involved. It may mean helping to tell a new story.

When a statement of belief is not only being stated but lived out what can be done? Fortunately, language tools that create and manipulate conflict can also be used to diminish it. The choice of words may bury the meaning and motivation of behavior. The intentional choosing of words may also uncover and reveal.

When I have a generalization dropped in my lap, my response is usually "true or untrue." I may find the belief statement to be offensive and simply walk away, shaking my head. I may try to explore why the person would think and say something "like that." Because of my own experience, I may find myself in agreement with the statement and feel aligned with the speaker. However, in each case, my response very well may not be to the real issue at all. Remembering the wife's statement, "They don't want my husband," just a response of either agreement or argument, does not result in an end to the conflict. "Yes, you are right" is incorrect. "No, you are wrong" expands the conflict to include me. Ignoring the statement and walking away offers no solution. Healing the conflict comes from first returning to the "event." And, the way that happens is through story.

We have always expressed ourselves best in story. Probably the first human verbal expression was a sound of warning. I do not know what the words sounded like but the meaning was "Run, you're about to be eaten!" Of course that prehistoric warning could have been left unspoken because I'd rather the other person be eaten than me. First came a sound to warn of impending danger. Then came a telling of story to give meaning and memory to what had happened. This verbal expression of an event is an effort for me to put the picture of the event that I have between my ears in between your ears too. I want you to see the event that I continue to see in my memory.

If a person flips through all the television channels, they may run across some educational T.V. and a program on the caveman and woman. Usually what is noticed in the inhabited caves are crude drawings. Scraped into the walls are not philosophical treatises on the nature of humanity. What is found is a collection of pictures about what happened once to someone. In humanity's earliest relationships, there was a need to warn and a need to share a story.

The ways we learn about something varies with different people. Some people learn best from what they see. Others learn most completely from what they hear. For someone else, learning comes from doing, touching and feeling. Everyone has a little of each but has one more prominent way to gain information. Story is a way to intertwine those ways together. We "hear" verbalized what is "seen" within the remembered experience about what was "done."

"Story is event wrapped in image and description."

When I am handed a statement of belief, it is

story that will help slice through the shell of hardened generalization, unwrap the bands of perception and power and reveal the event. It is then, from the event, that I gain insight. It is the event to which I respond.

My place in this process is to use language which invites the other person to tell their story. Just like words can help hide, words can also help reveal. I can also listen... really listen.

> *"Listening is the active engagement with another's experience, at the point of its initial verbal expression."*

My paying attention to what someone is saying doesn't begin when I get around to it several sentences into the conversation. I also do not pause my focusing on what is being said to judge the truth or inaccuracy of what is being said. And, I don't end my paying attention so I can sculpt a defensive or corrective response. Most people can instinctively tell if they are being listened to or if the other person is merely waiting on a pause in order to jump in with the perfect suggestion.

> *"Disclosure is not a down payment on advice."*

One of the quickest and surest ways to end the sharing of story is to jump in with advice. The listener wasn't there and isn't the story-teller. The listener cannot say "what they would do" or what the teller "should have done." To reveal something about an event in your life is to reveal something about yourself, which has been hidden. For the listener to quickly offer advice is to judge the teller as inadequate. Listening means using few words and those used do not claim ownership of the teller's story.

"Communication is the language of both physique and phrase, which binds us together, gives value and names us."

To clearly hear another's story, a careful listener will pay attention to the spoken language and also the posture of the teller. Does the teller look at or look away? Is the volume a whispered secret or a loud and excited anger? Is the body posture open and courageous or closed in fear? A shared story becomes a shared event, revealing a part of the teller that makes them who they are.

"Oh... I See!"

So, what can I say that will invite the telling of a story about an event? There is a way to help the story progress. There are words I can use to slice through the generalization, to wade through the perception, arrive at the event and even help choose a new story. This all begins when I remember that I am not inviting a presentation of logical facts or a well- argued defense of the stated belief. I am encouraging the telling of a story.

The telling of a story is to help the listener "see" what someone "did" at some time. In a more therapeutic model, after hearing the generalization, the listener would re-state or re-phrase what was just said. Sometimes it would be a "checking out" statement like, "What I heard you say is..." This method of "active listening" can be helpful in counseling. With it, the counselor establishes clarity of information and tries to give the person confidence they are being heard. Paired with this parroting back what was heard is an emphasis on uncovering and naming the "feelings" held by the speaker. These are all positive things. This is a basic method that is widely used. The process is moved along and concluded with the proclamation "I understand." However, there can be problems with this method. If I make a statement which is clear and important to me, is it diminished or devalued when the listener re-states it in a different way? Using their own words may make sense to the listener, but that's not what I said! Changing the statement may make the information more clear but it may not lead to the reason for the statement, which is the goal.

The response "I understand" sounds wonderful on the surface. But, the last thing I may want to hear after 30 seconds of beginning to reveal what I have hidden is the listener say "I understand." When that happens, I am left thinking, "I have been trying to understand myself and this event for months, and you understand in 30 seconds. No you don't!" The same is true of the statement, "I know how you feel." No, you may know what "you have felt" in a similar circumstance. You may have a presumption of what "you would feel" when experiencing the same event. The response claims a knowledge not yet acquired. However meaning to be helpful, the statement centers on the listener and not the speaker. Rather than inviting the speaker to go deeper into the story, the listener's words may halt their journey together.

When I am handed a hardened generalization, I am looked to for a response. Drawn into the conflict, what will that response look and sound like? Without choosing simple agreement or defensive denial, what is helpful? What words can I use that will invite a telling of the story that reveals the event?

Telling a story is a verbal attempt to give another's memory photo to me. The speaker wants me to "see" what they see. The focus is upon the action of an event. Therefore, the most helpful language centers on "action and seeing." My use of specific words can spark a connection with the story-teller's most prominent way of experiencing life events. My words can make connection with the auditory, the visual and the physical doing.

First, I replace questions of "why?" "Why do you think that?" is a question that says "Prove to me why you are right in believing that!" It is a request which leads to personal defense instead of invitation toward story. Secondly, my words center on the "action word or phrase." When focusing on the action, it "diminishes the personal." Finally, the arrival at the beginning event is celebrated with "I see!" My chosen words connect with and then draw out what the person in conflict has to share so that I can see.

The progression of story is really a simple process and usable by anyone finding themselves in the middle of conflict. Remembering the goal of "seeing the other person's event," my introductory response to the statement of belief and generalization is "let's *look* at that," which is appropriate in a group setting. In a personal or individual setting, the best response would be "help me *see*" or perhaps "I want to *see* what you mean." The speaker and listener are connected through *"hearing about an event that is seen."*

However, in most circumstances, no introductory response is even necessary. The best response for me to make is to repeat back to the speaker their action word or phrase. In my repeating the word back, I use their spoken word exactly. I do not change the word to make it more grammatically or politically correct. I do not change the word into my language and what I think they mean. It is important that I do not add any additional words to the word or phrase being reflected back. The one making the generalization needs to hear exactly what they said in order to connect cleanly back to the event.

Because I am wanting to uncover the event, I also eliminate any personal reference in my response. I do not include any names, groups or use unidentified "them, they, etc." To include the personal takes focus away from event and helps keep the generalization in place.

The speaker most usually will then restate what they first said either exactly or in slightly changed form. When I hear the words repeated, my response is exactly the same. I say back to them the action word or phrase just as it was said to me. This give and take may happen several times with only slight variations in the action word or phrase. The process may even begin to sound unproductive or even silly, but the words of the speaker will begin to change. The speaker wants the listener to "get the picture" and will begin to reveal more of the details of the event.

When the verbal exchange of exact words extends beyond two or three times energy may need to be added to the conversation. All I need to do is change the punctuation at the end of my response.

I may repeat the action word the first times as statements. After that, I may then change the inflection of my voice to create a question.

"They don't want my husband!"
   "Don't want..."
"No, that church doesn't want my husband."
   "Doesn't want..."
"The minister there just doesn't want him."
   "Doesn't want?"
"He just doesn't like him, not like he used to."
   "Not like used to?"
"He sure doesn't act like it any more."
   "Doesn't act like it..."
  "He used to always send him a birthday card"
   "Always send a card..."
"Not this year. Must not like him anymore."
   "Not like?"
"That's what he thinks and I guess he's right."
   "I see..."

I now can see the event. The speaker's memory photo is now mine also. While this does not end the conflict, the event which has been wrapped in perception and encased in hardened belief and generalization, can be addressed. Now I am dealing with reality.

"All they do is spend money!"
   "Spend money?"

"They just spend when they don't need to."
   "Don't need to..."
*"They hired some young guy that doesn't know
anything."*
   "Doesn't know anything?"
*" Yes, paying somebody that hasn't ever done
the job!"*
   "Hasn't ever done?"
*"No... and I even offered to help the younger
guys I work with how to do the job better."*
   "Even offered to help?"
   "OK, I see."

On most occasions, the progression of the story will be fairly short and the same action word or phrase will not have to be repeated numerous times. When it is, I may become impatient but it's important that I not slip into the process of direct questioning or "restating." That is when I will want to inject the phrase, "Help me see," or "Let's look at that." The key is to verbally focus on the action that has occurred to discover the event.

Teachers, counselors or even parents who work with even young children may find this method of focusing on story to be helpful. Many times, children will come to the closest adult with a "tattletale statement" about another child. On occasion, the child may use language that they only know a portion of its meaning. Perhaps the conflict has boiled over into a physical altercation that the adult has to handle. Arriving at the true ingredients of the conflict is helpful when deciding on any helpful response.

> *"Mark touched me inappropriately!"*
>> *"Touched inappropriately?"*
> *"Yeah, he slapped my bottom."*
>> *"Slapped..."*
> *"He was chasing me on the playground."*
>> *"Chasing you..."*
> *"We were running and he touched my bottom."*
>> *"Running..."*
> *"Well he was IT for tag."*
>> *"Oh, I see!"*

As the juvenile combatants are separated and checked over for medical needs, a story needs to be shared.

> *"I need you to help me see what happened."*
> *"He and I haven't gotten along for a long time."*
>> *"Haven't gotten along."*
> *"I'm fed up with his lying."*
>> *"Fed up... Lying?"*
> *"He says things to get people in trouble."*
>> *"Gets people in trouble."*
> *"He told some adults that my friends were drinking."*
>> *"Told?"*
> *"He told and they got in trouble."*
>> *"Oh, I see."*

Of course, in each case, there is more than one

side and perhaps more than one story. But by using carefully chosen words, the event may be uncovered and seen. When discovered, the real issue can become the focus and addressed.

I mentioned previously that I have shared this process in conflict resolution workshops. At the beginning of the workshop a large plastic Easter egg was examined and shaken, trying to guess what was hidden inside. Like most generalizations, it is hard to know what is at the center if only the outside is visible. No one ever guessed correctly. At the conclusion of the training, the egg was taken from the center of the table where it had sat. The outer shell was opened to reveal what appeared to be a tightly wound ball of string. Slowly the ball was unwound until it reveal what was had been hidden. When the center was revealed an audible "OH" was usually heard. What had been unseen, wrapped with bands and covered with a hard shell... was a key.

Steps Toward Change

Sometimes all change takes is an honest apology. Sometimes it is better just because it was heard. But most relationship healing occurs when "something is done." If the conflict began at the point of an event, owned or inherited, then an event may have the power to end it. Seeing the event in a different way changes the perception and power issues wrapping it. To add another act to the story changes the story.

An apology and explanation of the truth about the man who did not get his birthday card from the church changed the perception of the event. Exploring additional ways the worker can offer his knowledge to younger workers changes the focus of his relationship with the company. Beginning to find ways for new people to step into board leadership can change a stagnant inequality of power. Telling a "new story" becomes a possibility when the event-story is finally known.

Remembering that the focus is on event and action, there are four steps toward change. Each of these steps begins with a question. The question is asked of each of the conflicting sides.

"What do you want to see them do?"
This is a question that centers on the behavior of the other. This is not always as easy a question to answer as it sounds. Sometimes it has to be asked more than once in order for it to be taken seriously. If in an event, the behavior of another

began the momentum of conflict; then what event or behavior will stop it?

Working in mediation with juvenile offenders and adult victims, the behavior was often simple. Many times the victim wanted the offender to make a "sincere apology." Sometimes it was to do volunteer work in the community or school. With married couples, it may be as simple as "calling when you're coming home late" or "listen when I'm talking." The angry parishioner may want to see the minister "visit my mother in the nursing home." The female employee may want to see her boss "stop hugging me every morning." For a part of a community organization, it is to see the governing board "add a Hispanic member." The third-grader on the playground just wants to see "him stop calling me names and making fun of me."

The answers may be as varied as the people responding. Of course, sometimes the answer is not simple or helpful. "I want to see them jump off a cliff and die" is not a helpful answer! But it also does not end the question. Like leading them through story, from generalization to event, I may need to repeat the question more than once. What is most important is to identify a behavior or event change that can be seen. That action may help dilute the other actions that are a part of the story. "The cop that pulled me over had a smart mouth and treated me like I was stupid" can be diluted by "The cop called me by name and told me to be careful." A co-worker saying, "He really ripped me about the party I voted for" is balanced by "He asked me why I voted the way I did and then he listened." Seeing different actions creates different perceptions and changes beliefs.

"What can we do?"

The second question offers to create an event by which "we, together" prompt the first question. In most cases, an individual is reluctant to directly confront the other person or group involved in the conflict. Usually the hesitancy is due to a fear of the other's response or not wanting to "rock the boat" for the group. This fear is coupled with the hope that if ignored, the conflict will simply disappear by itself. But, we know that doesn't happen. Left alone, most conflicts will grow past a stage of easier management. So, it is essential to move through the apprehension and confront the issue directly. One person, alone, may be unable or unwilling to do what "we, together" have the strength to do. An offer to "stand with" another as they say what needs to be said and do what needs to be done, may strengthen resolve. Talking together about "how" someone needs to be confronted may add additional wisdom. The words used may be more carefully crafted and issue-focused rather than personal. The religious suggestion to "take someone with you to talk to a brother" is a wise one.

To this question, I need to have some suggestions before I ask. This does not mean that I give my answer first. It does mean that if no answer comes, I can offer "Can we see how you can tell this person...?" "What would it look like if we together went to see them?"

This is a question that can help to outline action. It probably will need a little nudge of suggestion to arrive at a verbal answer.

"What can I do?"

For there to be a "we" there must also be a "me." Again, I need to be prepared to suggest specific answers to the question. The other person may not know what I am able and willing to do to help. For that reason they may be hesitant to ask.

The answer is parallel to the previous question. What "we can do" is the result of what I am willing to do. "I can go with you when you go to talk." "I can help you decide what you want to say." "I can read the letter you write and tell you what I think." "I can buy you a drink to celebrate when you finish!" (OK, maybe not, but it sounded like a great idea when I wrote it!)

If the suggestion is made that I go instead of the other, I would hesitate saying yes. In some circumstances, the issue may so sensitive that a "representative voice" needs to confront on behalf of the victim . If there is a huge inequality of power which at first the "victim" cannot overcome, an initial confrontation by a third party may be necessary. However, the victim role can be discarded if the person can speak and confront for themselves.

Sometimes, power is necessary to face and re-balance power. This would be true in the case of conflict involving children and adults, job authority or intellectual abilities. Sometimes, it takes "we...including me" to change the balance.

"What will you do?"
Of all the questions asked, this one is the most important. This is the question that points to an answer that makes the difference. This is the question that is silently asked after each of the previous ones.

"What do you want to see *THEM* do?"
   "What will you do?"
"What can *WE* do?"
   "What will you do?"
What can *I* do?"
   "What will you do?"

Perhaps this final question puts responsibility where it truly belongs. What someone else needs to do to make a difference can be seen. But, the responsibility for changing the story is never just what the other person can do. Whether facing you in opposition or beside you in support, the other person only has a limited part to play.

Several *years ago, in a Midwest city, a labor dispute turned the community upside-down.*

The area was home to almost 30,000 people, most of whom had grown up together. When the about 500 workers at the largest of the local plants went on strike, it affected the entire community.

The first days of the strike were marked by face-to-face confrontation between striking employees and local law enforcement personnel. It was a time of anger, threats, accusations, name-calling and some isolated violence. Families and friends were divided into opposing camps. Tension seemed to define every relationship. But then, the atmosphere changed.

In the basement of a local church, an unreported on meeting took place. At the meeting were representatives of the striking union, members of company management and security, the County Sheriff and Under-sheriff and the Editor of the local newspaper. With the Editor moderating the meeting, the representatives of the opposing sides discussed perceptions and the use of power, and came to important agreements. The issues that were the reason for the strike were not settled at that meeting, but decisions about "how the strike would go about" were made. Over several hours, each group shared their beliefs, positions and needs. Each one agreed to what actions they would take to make the conflict as peaceful as possible until it was finally settled.

The strike did not end for many more days, but the event was changed. There was no more violence, almost no threats and greatly diminished public name-calling. There was still tension and anger but much of the personal had changed to focus on the issues.

A few days following the official end of the strike, some of the local churches joined together in a community worship service of "Peace and Healing." During the service, there were prayers, statements, readings and songs. However, the event of the night came at the end. As the service came to a close, participants were invited to make a gesture and say something to someone else in the crowd with who they felt estranged. During those moments, a stillness filled the room as no one moved. Then every head turned to watch as a uniformed deputy left his seat and walked across the crowded sanctuary. He made his way until he stood face-to-face with the leader of the strikers. The deputy offered his hand which was taken by the striker after only brief hesitation. The handshake then became a hug which then gave permission to a community full of broken relationships, to be healed.

Whether leading a group, listening to a friend, discussing politics on social media or confronting the blatant power of subtle prejudice, each person chooses their own words. With chosen words, boundaries are set and people are "put in their place." Our ability to share our words with an entire world has become fairly simple. Without any internal censor, beliefs of every kind can become the inherited event for a thousand nameless people. Those words can create conflict and carry it along, increasing its impact and power. Or, rightly chosen words can tell a different story and create healing.

Everything done up to this point, asks the question. All of the stories retold, asks the question. Everything that has been said, asks the question. Standing in a world swirling with created and manipulated conflict.... what will you do?

To listen more quietly ...
To observe more widely ...
To consider more deeply ...
Is to become aware.

Thank You!

Experiences with many people have shaped and molded the hopeful thoughts that created "At Word's Length." But the sharing of those observations and ideas was invaluably helped by a special few, to whom I am grateful. Their gifts of time and wisdom have been an encouragement during the entire process.

I am thankful to Robert Dees of Spiritual Health Associates and Dr. M.L. Niemeyer for their support, thoughtful reading and suggestions. For the positive reflection by the Honorable Roger Prokes, I am grateful. Essential was the editing work by Jennie Lamb.

Finally, I will always be thankful for all of those I have heard, who always had the right word at the right time.

www.ingramcontent.com/pod-product-compliance
Lightning Source LLC
Chambersburg PA
CBHW030023290326
41934CB00005B/455